WOKE
BOOKS

ORY IN PICTURES

OCUS ON

JAPANESE AMERICAN INCARCERATION

ELLIOTT SMITH
CICELY LEWIS, EXECUTIVE EDITOR

Lerner Publications ◆ Minneapolis

LETTER FROM CICELY LEWIS

Dear Reader,

Imagine being in an argument with a classmate and the teacher asks what happened. Your classmate tells their version of the story, but you don't get to share your version. Do you think this is fair? Well, this is what has happened throughout history.

CICELY LEWIS

This series looks at different events in US history with a focus on photos that help tell stories of people from underrepresented groups.

I started the Read Woke challenge in response to the needs of my students. I wanted my students to read books that challenged social norms and shared perspectives from underrepresented and oppressed groups. I created Read Woke Books because I want you to be knowledgeable and compassionate citizens.

As you look through these books, think about the photos that have captured history. Why are they important? What do they teach you? I hope you learn from these books and get inspired to make our world a better place for all.

Yours in solidarity,

—Cicely Lewis, Executive Editor

TABLE OF CONTENTS

Think critically about the photos throughout this book. Who is taking the photos and why? What is their viewpoint? Who are the people in the photos? What do these photos tell us?

Historically, the forced imprisonment of Japanese Americans was described as "relocation" or "internment." But many scholars argue "incarceration" (imprisonment) is a more accurate description. Which term do you think is more accurate? Why does word choice matter?

Tule Lake, the largest of the Japanese American incarceration camps

NATIONAL SHAME

DURING WORLD WAR II (1939–1945), THE US GOVERNMENT FORCED TENS OF THOUSANDS OF JAPANESE AMERICANS TO LIVE IN US INCARCERATION CAMPS. These camps are also known as internment camps, American concentration camps, relocation centers, or illegal detention centers.

Japanese Americans had to answer lists of questions while in incarceration camps. Two questions addressed loyalty to the US. If Japanese Americans answered both with yes, they remained at their camp. If they answered no, they were placed at Tule Lake in California, the maximum-security prison, for being disloyal.

Tule Lake opened in 1942 and stayed active throughout the war. It was the largest incarceration camp. Nearly nineteen thousand Japanese Americans were imprisoned there before it closed on March 20, 1946, six months after the end of the war. It was the last camp to close.

Tule Lake became a National Historic Landmark in 2006. Since 1969 activists have made pilgrimages to Tule Lake to bring awareness to what happened there. The shameful period in US history and those who survived this injustice would not be lost to time.

"I want people [to] know that such a thing could happen, and did happen, so it doesn't happen again. . . . No one stood up for us. Kids were removed from their classrooms and adults left their jobs, but no one said anything. We can't let that happen to anyone else."

—Satsuki Ina,
Tule Lake survivor

In 1942 a poster of Civilian Exclusion Order No. 5 declares that all Japanese people will be removed from the area in San Francisco.

CHAPTER 1
WHAT WAS JAPANESE AMERICAN INCARCERATION?

ON DECEMBER 7, 1941, THE JAPANESE NAVY BOMBED THE PEARL HARBOR NAVAL BASE IN HAWAII. This surprise strike directly led to the US entering World War II. It also led to increased fear and racism toward Japanese Americans across the country.

Before the war, the Federal Bureau of Investigation (FBI) kept a close eye on German, Italian, and Japanese individuals they thought were providing important or secret

Japanese Americans arrive at the Santa Anita Assembly Center in California on April 5, 1942, before being moved to incarceration camps.

information to enemies of the US. But after the attack on Pearl Harbor, the US government thought *all* Japanese Americans should be under suspicion for being enemies of the US, even though they had not committed any crimes.

In reaction to the fear, President Franklin D. Roosevelt signed Executive Order 9066 into law on February 19, 1942. This allowed US military forces to remove Japanese people from areas they set as military zones. The order applied to all Japanese people, whether they were Issei (first-generation immigrants to the US) or Nisei (second-generation American citizens born in America of Issei parents).

The next month, Public Proclamation No. 4 began the forced removal of Japanese American citizens. Many had less than forty-eight hours to make arrangements for their homes, land, businesses, and other property. The government then forced Japanese Americans into ten incarceration camps in the western half of the US. These camps were in remote, desolate parts of the country.

The Mochida family had to leave behind their nursery and greenhouses in California where they raised snapdragons and sweet peas.

All Japanese Americans were forced to wear identification tags while they were being moved to incarceration camps.

Japanese Americans wait to board trains for evacuation.

Executive Order 9102, signed by FDR, established the War Relocation Authority. The agency was in charge of imprisoning more than one hundred thousand Japanese Americans at these camps.

REFLECT

Japanese American citizens had to leave behind their property when they were imprisoned in incarceration camps. How would you feel if you had to leave behind your belongings or your home?

CHAPTER 2
LIFE IN INCARCERATION CAMPS

NCARCERATION CAMPS WERE SET UP LIKE MILITARY HOUSING, WITH LONG ROWS OF BUNK BEDS IN EACH BUILDING. There was very little privacy. Overcrowding, food shortages, and poor sanitation were common as the population grew.

Children went to school within the camps. Class sizes were large, and there weren't enough supplies for everyone. Children were taught math, English, and science. But the War Relocation

Authority also made children learn about American values and ideals in an attempt to teach loyalty to the US. Sports, especially baseball, were popular for children at the camps.

Most adults in the camps chose to work, although it was not required. They worked as doctors, custodians, cashiers, cooks, and more. At first, they were not paid for their work. Eventually, they earned between $8 and $16 per month. The Japanese Americans who worked at the camps earned far less than the white workers at the camps. For example, Japanese American teachers earned $228 per year while white teachers made at least $2,000 per year.

Children play at recess in Tule Lake.

A volunteer teacher teaches elementary school students at the Manzanar incarceration camp in California in 1942.

MEALTIME

Meals were served in large mess halls. Japanese Americans imprisoned at the camps waited in long lines for food, and the halls were often crowded.

Japanese Americans eating in one

Japanese Americans working in the kitchens at the Granada incarceration camp in Colorado in 1942

Kids and teens started eating with their friends instead of their families, showing a way family relationships changed. Hot dogs and canned meat were often served, along with other inexpensive foods.

A family in their housing unit at Tule Lake in 1942

Religion was an important element of camp life. Many of the Japanese Americans practiced Buddhism and Christianity.

Living in the camps affected relationships in many ways. Nisei and Issei had differing views on Japanese traditions, participation in activities such as baseball, and enlistment in the US Army. Different views created tension between the generations and in families.

Members of the One Hundredth Infantry Battalion, a racially segregated unit made up of Japanese Americans who fought in World War II

CHAPTER 3
CLOSING THE DOORS

SOME JAPANESE AMERICANS JOINED THE US ARMY AS A WAY TO PROVE THEIR LOYALTY TO THE US. The 442nd Regimental Combat Team was an army unit made up of Japanese Americans, many of whom were from Hawaii or were in the incarceration camps. The unit would go on to receive many awards for bravery or injury in service, including twenty-one Medals of Honor and more than four thousand Purple Hearts. It is the most decorated unit in US history for its size and service time.

REFLECT

How would you feel if you needed to prove loyalty to a country that you were already a citizen of?

Two high-profile cases of Japanese Americans reached the Supreme Court in 1944. Two years earlier, the FBI arrested twenty-three-year-old Fred Korematsu for refusing to go to an incarceration camp. Korematsu's lawyers argued that Executive Order 9066 was unconstitutional. In *Korematsu v. United States*, the court ruled in a 6–3 decision that the detention of Korematsu was necessary. Later that year, in twenty-two-year-old Mitsuye Endo's case, *Ex parte Endo*, all

Mitsuye Endo at the Central Utah Relocation Center, also known as the Topaz incarceration camp, in August 1944

Two young girls are among the Japanese Americans leaving the Granada incarceration camp to head back to their homes in October 1945.

Supreme Court justices ruled that the government could not keep Japanese Americans in incarceration camps.

These Supreme Court decisions and a shift in public opinion about the imprisonment of Japanese Americans led to the passing of Public Proclamation 21 on December 17, 1944. This released Japanese Americans from incarceration camps to return home beginning January 2, 1945.

All was not solved, however. Many Japanese Americans had lost everything as soon as they were taken to the camps. People without places to live filled the streets of cities like Los Angeles. Japanese Americans faced financial hardship and racism in their everyday lives.

RALPH LAZO

In 1942 Ralph Lazo took a stand. The seventeen-year-old Mexican American student, who had many Japanese American friends, voluntarily placed himself in the Manzanar incarceration camp in an act of solidarity. He was the only known non-Japanese person (and not a spouse of someone in the camps) to live at the camps. Later in life, he donated to causes that helped those who were kept in the camps.

Ralph Lazo (*center*) and

The Manzanar incarceration camp in June 1942

"It was wrong and I couldn't accept it," Lazo later said about the forced removal of Japanese Americans. "They were Americans, just like I am."

On February 19, 1976, President Gerald Ford (*sitting*) signs Proclamation 4417, which repealed Executive Order 9066.

CHAPTER 4

A PAINFUL LEGACY

OVER THE YEARS, THE US GOVERNMENT HAS MADE EFFORTS TO RIGHT THE WRONGS OF JAPANESE AMERICAN INCARCERATION. President Gerald Ford officially repealed Executive Order 9066 in 1976. In 1987 Congress introduced Bill H.R. 442, named after the World War II Japanese American regiment.

The following year, Bill H.R. 442 became the Civil Liberties Act of 1988, which President Ronald Reagan signed into law.

The law apologized for the incarceration and pledged $20,000 in reparations to every surviving US citizen who was forced into an incarceration camp. More than eighty thousand people received reparations.

In 2014 government administrations housed migrant children from Central America at Fort Sill, a military base in Oklahoma that was used as an incarceration camp for Japanese Americans in World War II. Seeing migrants kept there was a painful memory for many Japanese Americans. In 2019 many people, including survivors of incarceration camps, protested plans to house migrant children at Fort Sill.

On June 27, 2019, people protest the Trump administration's plan to hold migrant children at Fort Sill.

The disease COVID-19 spread around the world in 2020. It is believed the disease started in China. As the disease spread, racism and violence toward Asian Americans increased in the US. Many people wrongly blamed Asian Americans for the spread of the disease.

Japanese American incarceration is a dark chapter in American history. People continue to educate and inform others about it and make sure that it will never be forgotten or repeated. And many people continue to take a stand against racism.

> "Some people never talk about camp because of the pain of the experience or the shame and guilt they felt because they had been treated as disloyal or having done something wrong. It took me a long time to feel that it wasn't my fault, and that the government was responsible for it."
>
> —HIROSHI KASHIWAGI,
> Tule Lake survivor

TAKE ACTION

There are many ways to learn about and speak out against injustice. Here are some ways you can get informed and act:

See if you can visit a monument or marker where an incarceration camp was located. You can also browse the online exhibit of the Manzanar National Historic Site at https://www.nps.gov/museum/exhibits/manz/index.html.

Learn more about current immigration events and the groups that deal with immigration issues.

Check out the Japanese American Memorial in Washington, DC, at https://www.nps.gov/places/japanese -american-memorial-to-patriotism-during-world-war-ii .htm.

Research youth-led groups or movements that fight for causes you believe in, and learn how to get involved.

TIMELINE

FEBRUARY 19, 1942 — President Franklin D. Roosevelt signs Executive Order 9066, providing for the exclusion of any person from any area at the discretion of the military.

MARCH 1942 — The War Relocation Authority is established, and Public Proclamation No. 4 is passed.

DECEMBER 17, 1944 — Public Proclamation No. 21 is passed by the Western Defense Command, releasing Japanese Americans from imprisonment to return home starting January 2, 1945.

DECEMBER 18, 1944 — The Supreme Court, in *Ex parte Endo*, rules that "loyal" Japanese Americans could not be contained.

MARCH 1946 — Tule Lake is the last incarceration camp to close.

FEBRUARY 19, 1976 — President Gerald Ford repeals Executive Order 9066.

AUGUST 10, 1988 — President Ronald Reagan signs the Civil Liberties Act of 1988 to give reparations to Japanese Americans imprisoned during the war.

PHOTO REFLECTION

What is your reaction to this photo? How would you feel if you were forced to leave your home? Consider how your experience might be different from the experience of a friend or neighbor.

Take or draw a picture of where you live. What does your home mean to you?

GLOSSARY

GENERATION: a group of people who were born around the same time

IMMIGRANT: a person who lives in a country after moving from another country

INCARCERATION CAMP: a place where prisoners or minority groups are kept; also called an internment camp, relocation center, illegal detention center, or American concentration camp

INTERNMENT: a legal process where enemies of the US could be imprisoned during World War II

ISSEI: a Japanese term (pronounced ee-say) referring to the first generation of Japanese immigrants to the United States

MIGRANT: someone who moves from one place to another

NISEI: a Japanese term (pronounced nee-say) for the second generation of Japanese Americans born in the US of Issei parents

PILGRIMAGE: a journey, especially a long one, made to some sacred place

REPARATION: a payment made for damages or wrongful acts

SANITATION: the process of keeping places free from such things as dirt, infection, and disease by removing waste and trash

SOLIDARITY: a feeling of unity based on similar interests or goals

SOURCE NOTES

5 Taylor Weik, "Behind Barbed Wire: Remembering America's Largest Internment Camp," NBC News, March 16, 2016, https://www.nbcnews.com/news/asian-america/behind-barbed-wire-remembering-america-s-largest-internment-camp-n535086.

21 Carlos Aguilar, "The Little-Known Story of a Mexican-American Teenager Who Lived in a Japanese Internment Camp," Remezcla, June 1, 2018, https://remezcla.com/features/film/john-esaki-stand-up-for-justice-ralph-lazo-story.

24 Weik, "Behind Barbed Wire."

READING WOKE READING LIST

Atkins, Laura, and Stan Yogi. *Fred Korematsu Speaks Up*. Berkeley, CA: Heyday, 2017.

Attack on Pearl Harbor
https://kids.nationalgeographic.com/history/article/pearl-harbor

Chee, Traci. *We Are Not Free*. Boston: Houghton Mifflin Harcourt, 2020.

Executive Order 9066
https://americanhistory.si.edu/righting-wrong-japanese-americans-and-world-war-ii/executive-order-9066

Goldsmith, Connie. *Kiyo Sato: From a WWII Japanese Internment Camp to a Life of Service*. Minneapolis: Twenty-First Century Books, 2021.

Japanese American Internment
https://kids.britannica.com/students/article/Japanese-American-internment/631225

WWII Internment Timeline
https://www.pbs.org/childofcamp/history/timeline.html

Yamasaki, Katie. *Fish for Jimmy: Inspired by One Family's Experience in a Japanese American Internment Camp*. New York: Holiday House, 2019.

INDEX

PHOTO ACKNOWLEDGMENTS

Image credits: National Park Service, p. 4; Library of Congress (LC-USZ62-34565), p. 6; Clem Albers/National Archives, p. 7; Dorothea Lange/National Archives, pp. 8, 9, 13, 14, 21, 27; National Archives, pp. 10, 18, 22; Francis Stewart/National Archives, pp. 11, 16; John Cook/National Archives, p. 12; Tom Parker/National Archives, p. 15; U.S. Army Photo/Wikimedia Commons, p. 17; Hikaru Iwasaki/National Archives, p. 19; Gmatsuda/Wikimedia Commons (CC BY 3.0), p. 20; Ronen Tivony/Sipa via AP Images, p. 23.

Cover: Dorothea Lange/National Archives.

Content consultant credit: Ka Wong, Associate Professor of Asian Studies, St. Olaf
College

Lerner Publications Company
An imprint of Lerner Publishing Group, Inc.
241 First Avenue North
Minneapolis, MN 55401 USA

For reading levels and more information, look up this title at www.lernerbooks.com.

Main body text set in Aptifer Sans LT Pro.
Typeface provided by Linotype AG.

Editor: Brianna Kaiser **Designer:** Viet Chu
Lerner team: Martha Kranes

Library of Congress Cataloging-in-Publication Data

Names: Smith, Elliott, 1976– author. | Lewis, Cicely, editor.
Title: Focus on Japanese American Incarceration / Elliott Smith ; Cicely Lewis, executive
    editor.
Description: Minneapolis : Lerner Publications Company, [2023] | Series: History
    in pictures (Read woke books) | Includes bibliographical references and index. |
    Audience: Ages 9–14 | Audience: Grades 4–6 | Summary: "During World War II,
    Japanese Americans were forced to live in incarceration camps. Readers will examine
    the racism and fear that led to incarceration, what life was like in incarceration
    camps, and more"— Provided by publisher.
Identifiers: LCCN 2021044353 (print) | LCCN 2021044354 (ebook) | ISBN 9781728423463
    (library binding) | ISBN 9781728462868 (paperback) | ISBN 9781728461397 (ebook)
Subjects: LCSH: Japanese Americans—Evacuation and relocation, 1942–1945—Juvenile
    literature. | World War, 1939–1945—Japanese Americans—Juvenile literature. |
    Japanese—United States—History—Juvenile literature.
Classification: LCC D769.8.A6 S635 2023 (print) | LCC D769.8.A6 (ebook) |
    DDC 940.54/04—dc23/eng/20211012

LC record available at https://lccn.loc.gov/2021044353
LC ebook record available at https://lccn.loc.gov/2021044354

Manufactured in the United States of America
1-49184-49315-12/10/2021